DEFINITIVE GUIDE FOR INTERNATIONAL ECONOMY

JOSE-NICANOR PINILLA BARCELONA

DEDICATION

Special dedication to my wife Ana Miriam and my sons Joel and
Noah.

For more information: www.escueladelemprendedor.com

ACKNOWLEDGEMENTS

To all the teachers I have had since 1989, when international trade in Spain was not taken into account in the universities. Especially to the precursors of these subjects in Aragon, the International Business School (CESTE) and the University of Wales. I am grateful to all the students I have had for more than 20 years, who have taught me how to teach this subject. Thanks to the support of the School of the Entrepreneur, many teachers and professionals will be able to publish our knowledge in different business management subjects.

1. THE GROWTH OF INTERNATIONAL TRADE AND GLOBAL INVESTMENT

In the second half of the 18th century, international trade transformed the economy and society based on mercantilist theories and liberal principles. The industrial revolution and the dominance of the maritime market, which had the United Kingdom as its starting point, turned the country into the world's leading economic power. In this period of time, the foundations of the modern international economy were consolidated: capitalism, originally commercial, became industrial capitalism. In order to open up markets for the new industry, barriers and obstacles to trade previously set up to safeguard trade with the colonies were removed. Already in the 19th century, liberalism, based on the theories of comparative advantage and division of labour, overcame protectionist behaviour. It was thought that free trade would make countries better off in the face of protectionism. However, due to an imbalance in policy and wars from the end of the 19th century to the middle of the 20th century, the situation became protectionist again. It is in 1945 until today, when the phase of sustained growth of world trade begins, which has led to a moment in which the international political-economic context influences business decision making.

This movement has a significant impact on multinationals, whose activities (exports, foreign currency financing, foreign investment, etc.) depend on changes in the international economic environment. For SMEs, on the other hand, the concept of openness and liberalisation takes on a different meaning, as it implies greater competition in their domestic market, which forces them to specialise and seek new markets abroad.

The development of the more industrialised countries has led to an increase in the consumption of raw materials and semi-processed products. The growth of commodities has outpaced the growth of production. In a global market, the interaction between countries is becoming closer and closer. We can speak of the "butterfly effect".

> The "butterfly effect" means that an economic, social or political change can take place from any corner of the planet. Subsequently, and more or less immediately, it will end up affecting the rest of the world.

There is a constancy in the world economy (within this capitalist economic system) that developing countries, as they increase their productivity, increase their foreign trade in relation to industrialised countries.

At present, countries such as China have achieved economic growth of more than 10% per year. This means that they need to consume natural resources and raw materials to the nth degree, either to develop exports or to favour domestic demand.

Among the reasons for this increase, which is underpinned by international economic activity, are the following:

- ➤ **Political and economic stability**. With the Bretton Woods agreements in 1946, which created the International Monetary Fund and the World Bank, and the General Agreement on Tariffs and Trade in 1947, the foundations were laid for a new international economic order. Regulations on exchange rate variation are established, systems of cooperation and financial aid to the least developed countries are put in place, and the elimination of barriers to world trade is being negotiated.
- ➤ **Development of transport and telecommunications systems**. Today's means of communication and transport systems are very fast, so that distances have become an unimportant component of international business.
- ➤ **Technological change and technology transfer**. The technological developments that have taken place since 1960 have led to an increase in the size of companies in order to be competitive, thus forcing them to internationalise.
- ➤ **Legal certainty**. The large economic blocs, such as MERCO-SUR, NAFTA or the EU, have made it possible to develop an international market with less legal uncertainty, as multilateral agreements favour a more secure legal framework. As for trademarks and patents, it is easier and quicker to register the former, although emerging countries such as China are implementing unreliable registration systems for the moment.

Visit www.oepm.es

Before registering a trademark it is advisable to check whether it is available on this website.

- ➤ **Homogenisation of consumer tastes**. Due to the speed at which communication flows, especially through the media and the Internet, consumers seem to have similar tastes in terms of purchasing attitudes. Another reason has been the massification of large multinationals in terms of their advertising policies, however, not only is national identity being lost, but market segmentation is becoming greater and more specific.
- ➤ Niche markets have increased with respect to specialisation, although their target population is quantitatively decreasing.

➢ **Global competition and strategy**. One of the ways to compete in the international market would be to establish a planning strategy in terms of investment and costs taking into account economies of scale. A small company can develop an internationalisation process where it will have to invest, however, the standardisation of its processes in the international market together with the potential of a global market will reduce its unit costs, thus optimising its investments.

The internationalisation of the economy entails the following changes:

➢ Companies sometimes forgo investment in the domestic market due to saturation in favour of international expansion.
➢ The continuing emergence of industrialising countries encourages attempts to trade in these countries. Obviously, companies from developed countries such as the United States, Germany and the United Kingdom have better infrastructures and business culture to access these markets.
➢ The emergence of investor countries such as Japan allows its companies to overcome all kinds of barriers and restrictions that they had previously faced.

> In 2011, the New York City Council has just chosen the automotive company Nissan as the supplier of its legendary taxis. Who would have imagined it a few years ago?

➢ New configuration of the geopolitical map with the emergence of zones of influence such as ASEAN, which each year adds more countries such as China and Japan. We can safely state that China is today the country with the most productive foreign investment in the world and that it has become one of the world's three leading economic powers. In addition to Southeast Asia, there are other nations that are developing steadily, such as the BRICs (Brazil, Russia, India and China).

2. THEORIES OF INTERNATIONAL ECONOMICS

Theories of international economics try to explain why countries trade goods and capital movements with each other.

> All the flows generated by this exchange can be analysed through trends and patterns that help companies plan their strategies.

2.1. ADAM SMITH'S THEORY (ABSOLUTE AND COMPARATIVE ADVANTAGE)

Adam Smith presented the advantages of free trade in *The Wealth of Nations* (1776), but merely stated that goods would be produced wherever costs were lowest. In this work he also put forward the theory of absolute advantage, which provides the first theoretical explanation of international trade. According to his reasoning, if there were no trade barriers, each country would specialise in those products in which it had an absolute advantage over other countries. Productive resources (labour and capital) would be consolidated in those sectors in which the country has competitive advantages over others; costs would fall due to the action of economies of scale. The result would be international specialisation leading to lower costs and higher welfare for all components of trade.

> If to produce one unit of product X requires 10 units of labour in country A and 20 units in country B, and if to produce one unit of product Y requires 20 units of labour in country A and only 10 units in country B, then both countries can gain by trading. If these countries exchange the two products in a 1:1 relationship (one of product X for one of product Y), country A would get one unit of product Y with only 10 labour units, but if it were to produce it itself, it would have to use 20 labour units.

This theory is still useful today, since industries will be profitable according to the reduction they obtain in production costs.

2.2. DAVID RICARDO'S PRINCIPLES OF POLITICAL ECONOMY AND TAXATION

David Ricardo's *Principles of Political Economy and Taxation* (1817) laid the theoretical foundations that explain the advantages that countries can achieve through international trade. He adds to Adam Smith's theory that, if one country has an absolute advantage over another in the production of two goods, there are advantages in specialisation, since its advantage will be greater in one good than in the other. This is the theory of comparative advantage; for comparative advantage to exist, there must be at least two countries producing two goods. The difference between the production costs of one good is contrasted with the ratio of the other good in both countries.

The result of this theory is that each country will specialise in the product that is most profitable for its own consumption and for export, and will import those products that are not so economical to produce.

Comparative advantage demonstrates that free trade optimises the allocation of resources and is directed towards more productive returns, thus leading to a higher degree of welfare. The extinction of some sectors due to this trade liberalisation of imports is caused by an unfavourable economic environment (inflation, high wages, public deficit, etc.) and in many cases by poor business management.

To explain the theory of comparative advantage and the real terms of trade, Ricardo showed the exchange of cloth for wine that benefited Portugal and England, although he did not quantify this exchange, i.e. he did not refer to the international price of cloth. Even if export costs were the same in both countries, in Portugal cloth could be exchanged for wine in the ratio 90/80, one metre of cloth for almost a litre and a half of wine. Whereas in England the ratio of cloth would be 1 metre of cloth for 0.8 litres of wine. The final price at which the exchange is made depends on the demand of each country for the products of the other, i.e. the real terms of trade (R.R.I.).

2.3. MILL'S THEORY

Mill was the one who explained how advantages are distributed among countries. He also formulated the international demand equation and the theory of reciprocal demand, which surpassed and corrected Ricardo's theory in certain respects. Mill's breakthrough is the study of how the benefits of trade will be shared between the two nations. To develop it, he based himself on supply-demand analysis and explained how the distribution of the gains from trade depended on the relative prices of the goods that a country produced. But since to determine these relative prices it is necessary to analyse the relative supply and demand of goods, Mill succeeds in including the analysis of international trade, based on comparative costs, as a particular case of his general analysis of reciprocal demand whose centre is the international demand equation.

Or, conversely, we can also understand that the general case is the theory of international values while the theory of domestic values is a particular case based on the full mobility of factors. In Mill's own words: *"The products of one country are exchanged for those of other countries at such values as are necessary in order that the total of its exports may exactly pay for the total of its exports. This law of international values is but an extension of the general law of value, which we have called the equation of supply and demand [...] So that supply and demand are but another way of expressing reciprocal demand"*. (Mill, J.S, 1978, p. 511).

> The international demand equation ensures that an equilibrium will be reached in international markets, thanks to "competition" between buyers and sellers, or the law of supply and demand, so that the price of the total goods that the importing country wishes to receive exactly matches the total goods that the exporting country wishes to send.

The most important conclusion to be drawn from Mill's analysis of international values is that the proposition *trade is beneficial* is unconditional. Therefore, it is not indispensable for a country to be competitive in order to benefit from international trade. And it is precisely in those passages in which Mill devotes himself to explaining why taxes, tariffs and other protectionist measures do not benefit the nations as a whole, where we find the strongest statements against any limitation to free international trade. For example, he criticises the usefulness of a tax on exports: *"If, therefore, international morality were rightly understood, such taxes would not exist, because they are inimical to universal wealth" (Mill, J.S., 1997)*. (Mill, J.S., 1997, p. 49) This is how the so-called classical theory of international values is shaped.

2.4. HECKSHER - OHLIN MODEL

Already in the 20th century, with Ohlin's *Interregional and International Trade* (1993), a significant advance in the theory of international trade took place. A "new" explanation came into play that complemented the theory of comparative advantage to give rise to the traditional or neoclassical theory of trade: the theory of factor proportions or the Heckscher-Ohlin model. According to this theory and in Ohlin's own words: *"...generally abundant factors are relatively cheap and scarce factors relatively expensive in each of the regions. Those goods which in their production require a good quantity of the former and a small quantity of the latter are exported in exchange for goods which use factors in the inverse proportion. Thus, indirectly, those factors whose supply is abundant are exported and those whose supply is scarcer are imported"*. (Ohlin, B, 1971, p. 98).

> Countries tend to import goods that are intensive in the factors in which they have a scarce supply and to export those that are intensive in the factors for which they have an abundant supply.

For the conclusions of the theory to be valid, a number of restrictive assumptions must be met, from the relaxation of which some of the conclusions of the new trade theories will be derived. These assumptions are:

- ✓ There are two countries, two goods and two factors of production (labour and capital).
- ✓ Goods are perfectly mobile between countries (there are no transport costs or impediments to free trade), while factors move freely between the two industries within each country, but cannot move from one country to another.
- ✓ There is perfect competition in goods and factor markets, which are completely empty at equilibrium prices.
- ✓ The production functions of both countries are the same, with constant returns to scale and diminishing marginal products for both factors.
- ✓ The technology available in both countries to produce both goods and their advances are instantly incorporated into the production processes at no cost.
- ✓ Agents' preferences are identical in both countries.

> This theory is a development that goes beyond comparative advantage, but it does not represent a radical modification of the principles of Ricardo and Mill. The causes that explain trade remain the same (countries are different and their productions complement each other), but the new model brings a solidity that, once formalised by Samuelson, became absolutely dominant doctrine in the field of economic theory.

It seems that the neoclassical model does not fully explain international trade today. The theory is in some respects weak in explaining international trade due to overly restrictive assumptions ves. Incorporating imperfect competition and increasing returns to scale into the analysis provides new explanations for why trade takes place, while considerations of technological externalities, oligopolistic concentration in certain industries and learning curves may justify trade policies other than *laissez faire*. Neoclassical theory understands international trade as a win-win game, rather than a struggle in which there are winners and losers. Of course countries will compete to conquer new markets in order to sell their products there, but to see international trade as a war in which we must protect our markets and defeat the enemy (the other countries) would, according to the traditional theory of international trade, be a mistake.

With respect to David Ricardo's theory of comparative advantage, in which he said that labour is the only resource for the production of goods and that labour costs would be decisive for productive specialisation, we could qualify this theory by saying that there are countries that export goods not because production is greater, but because there are other factors such as raw materials or capital. We can cite the case of oil-producing countries (Saudi Arabia or Venezuela).

In general, countries with a lot of cheap labour have a tendency to export low value-added goods, as is the case in China or India. The costs and prices of goods produced in a country are different because each good requires a different mix of production and supply.

Hecksher and Ohlin tried to explain that there are only two productive resources. In a hypothetical market in equilibrium, each country would tend to export those goods that are intensive in the productive factor for which it has the greatest supply in relation to another factor, such as grain, which requires thousands of hectares and has a low production cost. Therefore, countries with large areas of cultivation of this product have a competitive advantage over the others.

When export prices in a sector rise, they experience large profits based on the use of factor-intensive goods with high turnover. In practice, some countries with cheap labour export labour-intensive goods, but this can also apply to countries with capital-intensive goods. The latter are less frequent. These findings are known as Leontieff's evidence, which can be summarised as follows:

➢ Work is different in each country, depending mainly on the education system, the evolution of working conditions, etc.
➢ Capital is heterogeneous. Many multinationals can develop different production systems in their country of origin and in the countries to which they relocate their production subsidiaries.

2.5. BRANDER AND SPENCER THEORY

James Brander of the University of British Columbia and Barbara Spencer of Boston College developed a model that sought to explain how governments of nations where firms operating in oligopolistic markets are located may have incentives to pursue an active and aggressive trade policy in order for the domestic firm to capture the largest possible market share (at the limit of becoming a monopoly), thereby increasing national welfare by increasing the profits of domestic firms.

> This model, the most famous and widespread of those relating to strategic trade policy, has a spectacular result, as well as being astonishingly simple and rigorous.

The authors' initial exposition is not based directly on a game-theoretic approach, but the clarity and cogency provided by such an approach has meant that, in its diffusion beyond the initial articles, the game-theoretic approach has displaced the graphical-mathematical one. We will now present the model in its game-theoretic version and then present a graphical approach to it.

Suppose there is an industry in which, in the absence of perfect competition, there is a market failure. This firm is a global duopoly, where a domestic firm (firm B) and a foreign firm (firm A) operate. As we are in an imperfectly competitive firm in this industry there will be extraordinary profits, i.e. the profits that can be achieved in this industry are above those that would be obtained in any other possible investment, for the same level of risk. Companies will try to capture the largest possible share of profits, as they are profit maximisers. There will be international competition to capture them. Suppose also that both firms sell their products in a third market that is neither country A nor B (where A and B are located respectively). In principle, there is no reason to assume that one of the firms will be able to capture a higher amount of profit if they start from equal situations. Continuing with the previous example, the game results matrix, it shows the profits or losses that both companies can obtain depending on how they behave. We are faced with a situation in which we must analyse the strategic behaviour of both companies.

Consider companies A and B as producers of commercial aircraft. This implies that we are dealing with an industry with high barriers to entry, where the good produced has a very high price and more technology is used (which in turn can have important externalities). Suppose that both companies are able to produce a new aircraft that is in demand by a multitude of airlines, a 200-passenger jet that incorporates new technology, these two companies are the only ones in the world able to produce it. For simplicity's sake, suppose the firms must decide whether to produce or not in the market; there is no in-between.

This example tells us that if both companies produce the aircraft they will both incur a loss of 10, meaning that there is not "enough room" for two companies in this market. If company A produced and company B did not, then company A would take all the profits 100 and B would take nothing and vice versa. And if neither produces, the result is 0. In principle, neither company would produce the plane, as they would risk making a loss. But since the plane is not going to remain unbuilt, let us suppose that it is company A that has an initial advantage, which consists of deciding before company B whether to produce or not. In this case, company B will have no incentive to produce, once that company A enters the dominant strategy it will be the one that makes a profit of 100. Now let us consider that company B finds a way to produce more efficiently, thus reducing its costs by 20. We will have to add 20 to the results that B obtains when it enters the market.

We observe that there is a dominant strategy for company B. By reducing costs, it will achieve an increase in its production capacity and therefore become more profitable. When company B's situation improves, company A would withdraw from the market because it thinks that company B has reached stability in the market. Another figure that could come into play would be the government that could subsidise company B, as it would be more than justified due to the increase in company B's profits, therefore, the government would increase tax collection. We can see that the government's intervention unbalances the initial advantage that the company had. This allows us to draw a number of conclusions that the government can subsidise domestic firms without any restrictions. Therefore, in international trade, which is apparently governed by multilateral WTO agreements, it will influence the imposition of sanctions or barriers to export subsidies. In practice, many countries do not respect these agreements and there is no sanctioning capacity either.

2.6. NEW THEORY OF INTERNATIONAL ECONOMICS

We have already seen the classical theories of international trade through comparative advantage, each country produces goods according to its differential advantage and through exchange they complement each other. The sum of these resources, labour and capital, determine the pattern of international trade. According to traditional theory, because countries complement each other in terms of production, all trade should be a quasi-perfect exchange.

> Trade between EU member states increased to the nth degree after the establishment of the Customs Union.

As we can see, this example does not respond to Hecksher and Ohlin's model of productive complementarity between nations, but is an intra-industrial exchange.

The causes of high intra-industry trade in the more developed countries are economies of scale and the importance of value-added products. The advantages of increasing returns to scale together with the diversification of demand from more advanced countries have been instrumental in establishing new conclusions as to why trade takes place, as well as explanations of new advantages brought about by new international markets. In terms of welfare theory, international trade allows many of the goods that are demanded in a country and that have some functionality for its citizens to reach their hands. Without this exchange, welfare would be lower for the more developed economies. We can affirm that international exchange improves global welfare.

> A trade policy that obstructs free trade is detrimental to the welfare of citizens.

2.7. INDUSTRIAL ORGANISATION THEORY

Trade theories based on market imperfection are closely linked to industrial organisation theory as justifications for protectionism in general. In particular, strategic sectors, supported by an active industrial policy, are those with barriers to entry. We now turn to an explanation of the barriers to entry:

Barriers to entry. They are one of the requirements for considering a sector as strategic. The existence of these barriers makes a market competitively imperfect. Governments may encourage an active industrial policy that tries to shift profits to domestic companies. The absence of barriers is a symptom of competitive perfection.

> According to Bain, barriers to entry are those that allow incumbent firms to achieve extraordinary profits by raising the price above the competitive level without inducing new firms to enter the industry.

Bain points to four factors that define market imperfection:

- The existence of economies of scale. This is one of the most important elements for oligopoly markets to occur.
- Absolute cost advantages.
- Initial capital requirements.
- Product differentiation.

Barriers to entry reduce welfare because they create market power. They create strategic sectors, sectors with higher value added, when these sectors compete in the international market it is no longer so clear that entry barriers reduce national welfare, therefore, the government can regulate by subsidising domestic firms that compete internationally. We can distinguish two types of entry barriers:

- Those that arise naturally. As are companies that exercise a monopoly (the case of Telefónica).
- Those that arise as a consequence of strategic actions, either by groups of companies or by the government.
- Economies of scale. The existence of increasing returns to scale is essential for two reasons:
- They are the fundamental cause of the existence of intra-industry trade. As the neoclassical model explains, if we have two countries, one with an abundance of capital and one with an abundance of labour, and both have constant returns and operate in perfect competition, the pattern of trade corresponds to a country where there is only intra-industry trade.

A very similar situation occurs when there are increasing returns to scale (average costs decrease with increasing output) and the market for manufactures, instead of functioning in the form of perfect competition, functions in the form of monopolistic competition according to Chamberlain's model. In this case, intra-industry specialisation occurs. This happens because it is not in the interest of any of the countries to fully satisfy the diversified demand for manufactures made by their citizens, because if they do so they do not take advantage of economies of scale.

> With increasing returns to scale, it is in the interest of firms to specialise in particular goods and to meet domestic and international demand for those manufactures.

Therefore, what happens is that, given the diversity of demand for manufactures in both countries, country 1, despite being a net exporter of manufactures, will also demand manufactures produced in country 2, giving rise to intra-industry trade. In turn, consumers in both countries benefit for two reasons:

➢ They enjoy a wider choice of products (close substitutes).
➢ They pay a lower price for them as a result of cost reductions for companies that take advantage of increasing returns to scale.

In short, the introduction of economies of scale into the model expands the explanations of why trade takes place: inter-industry trade stemming from comparative advantage. However, which country produces which manufactures, and how much intra-industry trade accounts for the total, remains undetermined. We only know that, even if both countries have identical factor endowments, there will be intra-industry trade and that the more similar these endowments are, the more intra-industry trade will represent a higher percentage of total trade. Economies of scale would in this case be the fundamental explanation of trade while comparative advantage would explain virtually nothing.

The second reason is that they cause barriers to entry. Economies of scale lead to barriers to entry.

> Economies of scale or increasing returns to scale exist when, when multiplying all factors of production by a quantity, output is multiplied by a number greater than that quantity.

Industrial concentration, mergers and acquisitions, or the rapid increase in production by a firm in its early years even when incurring losses (dynamic economies of scale), are often strategically motivated by firms to take advantage of economies of scale, i.e. to reduce their unit costs by increasing production. But when firms do this, they are at the same time erecting barriers to entry into the industry for potential competitors. This happens because if a firm is able to reduce its average costs by increasing output, its potential competitors, who do not have such a large installed capacity , will not be able to put their products on the market at a competitive price.

Industrial concentration is often the result of strategic actions by firms. But economies of scale as a cause of entry barriers seem to arise naturally because it is undeniable that most industrial sectors show increasing returns to scale. Moreover, the logic of the capitalist system seems prone to processes of capital concentration in order to take advantage of this fact. In industrial production processes, the expansion of production plants makes it possible to reduce unit costs.

In such situations, industrial policy can either try through regulation to reduce the inefficiency of situations that cannot be solved (e.g. regulating prices in markets that are natural monopolies), or to promote competition by combating concentration, abuses of dominance, horizontal agreements and any other similar practices to curb concentration, which is particularly pronounced in sectors such as information technology.

Investment in R&D. It is essential for the increase of consumer welfare and for the development of the capitalist system because it is necessary to increase productivity, reduce costs and invent new products continuously in order for the system to sustain itself. But the public or private good character of the different stages of research, the importance of its external effects, the effectiveness of patent systems and thus the level of copying of innovations from one company to another is less clear. A major controversy arises as to whether R&D investment should be public or private.

Three categories of research are usually distinguished:

- Basic. Aimed at obtaining scientific knowledge that is not oriented towards a specific practical end or application.
- Applied research. This includes work with a specific practical purpose based on basic research.
- Research for development or R&D. It results from the use of the work of previous research to exploit new products or processes or to improve existing ones.

The first of these categories, which is usually carried out in universities or other centres of knowledge production, but not in private companies, takes the form of a public good, and as such, in the absence of public intervention, there is a tendency towards insufficient production. In this first stage, it is logical to think that the state should finance part of the research to correct this market failure, even more so if we take into account the positive external effects it has for the economy as a whole. But in the other two categories, research no longer fits the definition of a public good, and moreover, throughout history, these innovations have come from within private companies.

We must then ask: is there insufficient production of applied and developmental research, should the state fund this research through subsidies to private companies, or which market structure presents the most incentives for innovation?

Proponents of strategic trade policy argue that the state should maintain an active stance by both funding research conducted by private firms and promoting the creation of both public and private institutions that foster knowledge creation. They argue that private firms do not have sufficient incentives to invest in R&D the amount that would be socially optimal, and therefore, especially given the large profits of high-tech industries, their positive externalities and the aggressiveness of international competition, it is in the interest of the economy as a whole that industrial policy should be concerned with the promotion of high-tech investment. The underlying argument here is, once again, that of barriers to entry. If domestic firms are able to develop significant innovation through government support for R&D subsidies, they will be able to block entry by potential foreign rivals through cost reductions or the development of entirely new products resulting from research.

The mere announcement that the government is going to subsidise a domestic firm's R&D investment in the development of a new product could be enough to "intimidate" its potential competitors abroad and cause them to withdraw from the development of that good. In this way, the level of R&D investment provided by the government acts as a signal to the market, making domestic firms perceived by their competitors as more powerful.

Because of the importance of historical accidents in the creation of comparative advantages, it is indispensable for the state to support investments in markets with high growth potential, but whose investments are subject to high risks that companies are not willing to take on their own. These risks stem both from the possibility of failure of some investments and from the impossibility for companies to appropriate the full benefits of such investments due to ineffective patent systems.

It is well known that Microsoft's Windows system, today the absolute leader in the computer industry, is a copy of the Machintosh system.

The argument used by advocates of strategic trade policy to argue for increased R&D subsidies is based on the assumption that there are or will be windfall profits in high-tech sectors and that it is in a country's interest that these profits go to its own rather than to foreign competitors. It is therefore useful to analyse whether this view of the world market as a "struggle between countries" in which companies appear as representatives of those countries is correct. The international economy in imperfect competition. Since the Second World War, foreign trade has increased in those industrial countries with similar factors of production. Today, one third of international trade is made up of the market between OECD countries. This situation has given rise to other theories that are integrated into the classical analysis, to demonstrate the existing market between nations in which there is a state of imperfect competition more in line with the current market reality. In the following, we will examine the main approaches to this situation.

2.8. INTERNATIONAL TRADE AND ECONOMY OF SCALE

To begin with, we will have to differentiate between national and international economies of scale:

☐ National mergers take place within the company and are related to the size of the factory. The reason for these is cost reduction due to specialisation or organisational improvements.

☐ International are outside the company and relate to the size of the global market. They correspond to a given sector in which all companies, both domestic and foreign, are included. The source of economies of scale in this case is a component external to the company itself: the sector in which it operates.

The main result of economies of scale is that, as a result of the increasing returns that firms are able to achieve, production can be centralised in a small number of large firms, giving rise to an oligopoly of supply. In such a market, the profits do not accrue to a single firm as is the case in a monopolistic market, but the desired situation of perfect competition does not arise.

In a sector where firms present a product that the public perceives as different from the rest of the competition, not only external economies of scale, but also monopolistic competition takes place. As a result of this specialisation, each firm will have a similar pricing policy to the monopolist and will have the possibility to achieve economies of scale by projecting its market outwards.

Explanatory theories of economies of scale show that trade relations will take place between countries even in the assumed situation where they all have the same productive resources in equal proportions and will be used to produce the same amount of goods in all industrial sectors. Due to economies of scale, those countries that enjoy higher productivity will gain competitive advantages in the manufacture of certain goods, which as a general rule are those in which they tend to specialise.

> A clear example of international trade based on economies of scale are those companies that, due to an oligopolistic situation in their sector, have been forced to outsource their processes to other countries in order to achieve higher and better productivity.

2.9. INTERNATIONAL TRADE AND TECHNOLOGY

Posner's model established that a company with a technological advantage in the production of a good would tend to export it. Under this premise, as soon as the competitive advantage becomes known in the international market, this advantage tends to become obsolete, although new inventions and cutting-edge technologies will appear that will renew the market. These innovations tend to be concentrated in certain sectors, and are organised into industrial groupings called clusters. This would bring cost savings, as they share the same resources.

> An industrial cluster is a grouping of companies and auxiliary companies in the same sector, located in the same geographical area.

In terms of international trade flows, there are studies on the importance of technology in various sectors and different countries, as in the case of Soate. Some of the conclusions reached in his studies were that the proportionality of patents is directly related to a country's competitiveness. In Europe, we can cite the case of Germany. For example, in biotechnology patents, there are more than 7,000 patents registered in the world. Germany is the country with the most registrations (about 1369) followed by the United States (with more than 2500).

Another study by Fagerberg shows that the countries with the highest growth in GDP and exports have been those with the highest growth in technological factors and investment capacity.

> Germany and Japan grew exponentially in GDP and exports after World War II, as their unit labour costs rose faster.

Today, this difference in technology means that there are countries whose industries specialise in low value-added products, while other countries with higher technology provide products with very high added value.

2.10. INTERNATIONAL TRADE AND PRODUCT DIFFERENTIATION

One of the characteristics of international trade in recent times has been the increase in simultaneous import and export trade in the same country of products belonging to the same sector. This is the case of the automotive industry. According to Linder, the cause that most influences international trade in manufactured products is the structure of demand in terms of the characteristics and qualities of the product consumed in a country. When consumer tastes are homogenised, international trade in manufactured goods will be greater. Apparently, companies in the same sector produce goods with similar characteristics, especially in terms of tangibles (physical properties and qualities), but the differentiation lies in the intangibles (quality of service, brand, guarantees, etc.). Therefore, this means that price is not such an important variable.

In a globalised market with very similar tastes, it is difficult to stand out with a specialised product. However, one of the keys to success in international trade is precisely to try to standardise the product and its processes and at the same time specialise in a specific market niche.

2.11.   INTERNATIONAL TRADE AND PRODUCT LIFE CYCLE

R. Vernon's (1966) famous analogy has been widely used and continues to be useful when thinking about an organisation's strategy. Knowing what we are good at and where we are active is important, but it is advisable to analyse the dynamics of our market in detail, simply because it is constantly changing and a good strategy, let us remember, is always linked to the life cycle of the company's products - services - markets. We do not compete in the same way in a market that is growing, mature or declining (García and Sabater, 2004).

The first phase of the product life cycle begins with the manufacture and design of a new product in order to sell it on the domestic and international market. In later stages, some industrialised countries decide to relocate to developing countries in order to lower labour costs. From these countries they export to the international market. One of the reasons for offshoring would be to increase a product's investment in R&D&I in order to be competitive and that cheap labour will therefore facilitate the competitiveness of such products. However, it has been shown by several countries (Germany and Japan) that a highly skilled, albeit expensive, workforce also makes it possible to be competitive. It all depends on the added value given to the product at source. The life cycle model of a manufactured product goes through four main stages:

Introduction: This is the first stage where a product is created and innovated. Manufacture and subsequent marketing are carried out in the country of origin. This is because the decisions taken in these companies respond to the exhaustive knowledge of their domestic market. There is also a direct link between production and domestic consumer demand. Innovation usually takes place in more developed countries, as they have sufficient demand for new goods from a high purchasing power market segment. It is difficult for a developing country to have a middle class with sufficient purchasing power to make the demand for these products profitable. In more industrialised countries we find that the population has a higher educational and technical level to value novel products.

This first part is very labour-intensive in terms of the production process. Although standardised processes are being implemented for subsequent mass production, it is still too early to say that mass production is achieved at this stage. Companies that tend to invest in an innovative process for their product have a better chance of starting to open up markets.

Growth: In this stage there is an increase in demand from the domestic market, as well as from exports. Therefore, in terms of production, companies start to increase their volume and turnover. When the company starts to expand internationally, the potential markets obviously increase. The company must carefully analyse the logistics and customs conditions of each market (tariffs, taxes, technical barriers). This stage means mass production splendor and the company must invest in industrial machinery in order to be more competitive and to be able to serve large volumes of orders to various international markets. Competitors begin to appear and prices begin to fluctuate.

Maturity: The process of maturity means that the product has been massively accepted by the market and that there has been an increase in demand and producers in the same sector. An amalgamation of strategies appears to compete in that market, some focused on "bottom price" or specialisation where high prices can be maintained. Since we are in a very competitive stage, some companies are disappearing because they cannot withstand the price war. Some choose to delocalise their production subsidiaries, establishing joint ventures or joint ventures with foreign partners, and others decide to apply a higher added value to their products, which allows them to stay in the market.

> The lowest price that a company can give without making a loss is called the bottom price.

Decline: We have reached the last stage of the product cycle. In this stage, the good no longer appeals to the market because it has competitors that are more attractive to the consumer or are more innovative or of higher quality. The most industrialised countries begin to reduce their production and developing countries begin to require these products (EU and China, respectively).

3. BALANCE OF PAYMENTS

A country's balance of payments reflects the most comprehensive analysis of a country's international trade activity and flows with the rest of the world. It is an accounting document that records all transactions of different types between citizens, companies and institutions that carry out flows with the rest of the world during a given period of time, which is generally one year. For natural persons, the criterion of habitual residence in the country is used. For legal persons, all companies domiciled in the country are considered residents, as well as branches and subsidiaries of foreign companies.

We can also define the balance of payments as a statistical record whose importance consists in providing information about a country's financial flows abroad, foreign exchange movements and competitive capacity. Therefore, we are considering at all times three aspects: accounting, financial and economic. According to the International Monetary Fund's "*Balance of Payments Manual*", the balance of payments is defined as "a statistical statement summarising the economic transactions between a country's economy and the rest of the world". It is of vital importance for the central agencies of a nation. For example, central banks.

Spain: Banco de España.

France: Banque de France.

Germany: Deutsche Bundesbank.

The balance of payments is an accounting document whose function can be defined as a statistical record for the purpose of double-entry accounting of all economic and financial flows between residents of a given country and non-residents during a given period, usually a year, which we call a fiscal year. The balance of payments is compiled by the Banco de España, whose data are provided by the Tax Administration through the Single Customs Document (SAD) and through INTRASTAT (Intra-Community

Acquisitions and Deliveries). The central banks of each country provide their corresponding balances of payments to the International Monetary Fund. After analysing them and passing them through the sieve of its regulations, it publishes them in the Balance of Payments Statistics.

These transactions comprise exchanges of goods, services, income, transfers and transactions in financial assets and liabilities. Double-entry accounting requires all transactions to be recorded in two entries of the same amount, but in reverse: one in receipts or changes in liabilities, the other in payments or changes in assets.

The first item records the entry of foreign exchange into the country (export of goods). The second item records payments or outflows of foreign currency from the country (import of goods).

Each transaction, therefore, gives rise to two entries, one on the assets side and one on the liabilities side. The balance of payments implies a permanent equilibrium, whereby the sum of receipts must equal the sum of payments. The accounting document is divided into headings, items and headings.

The headings are summarised under four headings and include the three basic accounts:

- Current account.

- Capital account.

- Financial account.

- Errors and omissions.

3.1. CURRENT ACCOUNT BALANCE

If we were to make an analysis of international marketing, the current account would be the most relevant for a comprehensive analysis. It records the items relating to the operations of:

- Balance of goods and merchandise.

- Services.

- Rents.

- Current transfers.

The current account is the formation of its four component items or balances that give rise to the calculation of "sub-balances", such as the trade or services balance, which show the surplus or deficit or a balance of trade. Normally the indicator used is the trade balance. If we have a favourable balance, the current balance will allow us to lend and invest in international markets. In order to know the competitiveness of a country, we must analyse the goods and services account, i.e. the trade and services balance.

3.1.1. BALANCE OF TRADE OR BALANCE OF GOODS

The result of the material goods bought and sold by a country during a fiscal year in international trade is called the trade balance. The items that make up the balance of trade are exports and imports. Exports are the source of foreign exchange inflows and receipts, and imports are the source of payments for goods. It is considered an integral part of the balance of payments, namely the current account. Exports help to regulate payments in order to offset imports. They contribute to the economic growth and strengthening of a country. In a national economy, export growth neutralises inflation differentials.

Because we already have a market in the European Union, exports are considered to be trade with third countries. Therefore, trade in goods is subject to customs duties and taxes. All declared imports and exports are accounted for on a common basis. This basis pertains to the delivery terms of the INCOTERMS (International Commercial Terms). Exports are valued on FOB terms, as are imports, except if imports of goods are detailed from the country of origin, which will then be valued on CIF terms.

> FOB: Free on board. Value of the goods loaded on board the vessel at the port of departure.
>
> CIF: Cost, insurance, freight. Value of goods insured for 110% of their invoice value up to the port of destination.

3.1.2. SERVICES

This is the item that contains all receipts and payments transactions related to the provision of services between residents and non-residents of a nation. It includes a range of services:

☐ Tourism and travel.

☐ Transport and communications.

☐ Insurance.

- Construction.
- Financial and computer services.
- Cultural and recreational services.
- Government services.
- Business services (leasing, commercial, etc.).
- Licensing fees (royalties).

> The trade balance refers to exports and imports of tangible or tangible goods. The services balance refers to exports and imports of intangible goods, i.e. intangible goods or services.

Among the income from services rendered, we can list those provided by foreign companies, organisations and individuals. For example, all the tourists who come year after year to enjoy the Spanish beaches. We can also obtain income or expenses through freight in maritime transport, as well as goods insurance. In the case of Spain, we can highlight that the most profitable item in the balance of services is Tourism. The positive balance of this item has largely offset the deterioration of the trade balance.

3.1.3. INCOME

The income balance includes income and payments generated by workers' compensation and investment income, i.e. it includes investment income from assets invested in the country's economy and income of Spanish residents from their financial assets invested abroad (interest on loans, dividends, real estate rents, etc.). We will also include royalties from collections and payments of patents, trademarks and copyrights, as well as the wages of workers whose activity is carried out in a country of residence other than that of their nationality (seasonal and temporary expatriates).

3.1.4. CURRENT TRANSFERS

Includes all receipts and payments without any consideration between residents and abroad. A distinction can be made between private transfers (remittances from migrants residing abroad) and public transfers (development aid funds). Current transfers are distinguished from services in that they involve no apparent financial consideration, whereas in services the cost of the service involves the provision of transport, accommodation and food, in the case of a tourism service. In transfers, there is no consideration and can be called a balance of free services. They usually include transfers from public administrations with the European Union, aid to the Third World, payments to international organisations, remittances from migrant workers, grants to citizens who go abroad, artistic and scientific awards, etc.

3.2. CAPITAL ACCOUNT BALANCE

This balance includes general government grants and capital transfers and transactions in assets and materials.

➢ Capital transfers. These basically include inflows from the European Union, capital transfers from the private sector and those of public administrations with the European Union, earmarked for structural improvements in industrial and environmental projects.
➢ ERDF (European Regional Development Fund).
➢ EAGGF (European Agricultural Guidance and Guarantee Fund).
➢ Acquisition/disposal of intangible assets: Purchase and sale of intangible assets.
➢ Non-produced intangible assets (land, subsoil, etc.).
➢ Intangible assets (patents, trademarks, copyrights, etc.).

Since investment goods are recorded in the income balance, they should be considered as financial capital. To account for transactions between residents and non-residents in the current account and the capital account, there is a receipts column and a payments column. The system used is the double entry system, whereby each transaction gives rise to two entries: one in the income column and one in the payments column.

✓ Income is considered to be income:
   o Exports of goods and services.
   o Income of Spanish residents abroad.
   o Current and capital transfers received.
✓ They are considered payments:
   o Imports of goods and services.
   o Income of foreign residents in Spain.
   o Current and capital transfers sent.

3.3. FINANCIAL ACCOUNT BALANCE

It is the counterpart of the current and capital accounts (except errors and omissions) whose function is to record financial transactions. It records all changes in financial assets and liabilities in net flows between residents and non-residents.

> Changes in assets involve the country's investments abroad, i.e. payments made by residents for the purchase of assets from non-residents, as well as the country's disinvestments abroad, equivalent to the proceeds from their sales and redemptions. Liability changes involve foreign investment in the country, i.e. income earned by non-residents on the purchase of assets from residents, as well as foreign disinvestment in the country, equivalent to the payments derived from their sales and redemptions.

The financial account is structured in four balances, differentiated by the type of assets and liabilities in which the investments are materialised:

Direct investments. The investor takes a stake that allows him/her to effectively influence the control and management of the company. This must not be less than 10% of the capital or be a sufficient condition to sit on the board of directors. The investor's objective is to obtain a high return over time in the company in which he invests, gaining control over the management of its activities. This section also includes the acquisition of real estate.

Portfolio investments. Acquisitions of securities that do not constitute direct investment, as no control over the investee company is sought. Examples include shares and units in investment funds, bonds and debentures, money market instruments and derivatives (futures and options).

Other investments. They affect changes in financial assets and liabilities such as loans between residents and non-residents, except those granted by companies to their subsidiaries, trade credits with a maturity of more than one year and demand or term deposits with financial institutions.

Changes in reserves. They contain liquid assets (gold, foreign exchange and IMF positions), which are considered available for use by a country's central authorities to finance balance of payments imbalances or to minimise their interventions in the foreign exchange market.

Transactions in the financial account are recorded in the columns for changes in assets and liabilities. Foreign investments in Spain are recorded in the column for changes in liabilities and investments abroad in the column for assets. Increases in reserves are recorded in the column for changes in assets and decreases in the column for changes in liabilities.

3.4. ERRORS AND OMISSIONS

The imbalance or difference derived from the totals between current and capital account receipts and payments is recorded, giving a positive or negative balance. The main function of this account is to ensure that the result of the sum of the different items is equal to 0. The significance of this account is specified in three analytical aspects:

The accounting significance that lies in the permanent equilibrium guaranteed by the application of the double entry method: The sum of receipts plus change in liabilities has to be equal to the sum of payments plus change in assets.

The financial significance reflected in the financial account that highlights the country's debit or credit position vis-à-vis the outside world:

Increase in financial assets: increase in creditor position.

Increase in financial liabilities: increase in debit position.

The economic significance that declares the real situation of a country in its external relations, embodied in the current and capital account. Both accounts are those that record the income and payments for income-creating operations during a specific period, therefore, the result that reflects the sum of the current and capital accounts is of utmost importance for the economy of a country and shows the financial capacity of that country.

Many of the industrialised economies are chronically in deficit, such as the United States. While import surpluses are cheap due to excessive domestic consumption, exports are proving uncompetitive and stagnating. In fact, imports are being financed by borrowing and savings from other economies are underpinning the financial need. The situation of the US economy is under severe stress and forecasts, despite a global GDP of $14.6 trillion in 2009, indicate that the prosperity of the world's leading power is threatened with fatal shocks in the coming years.

The budget deficit for 2009-2010 in the United States was $1.57 trillion, which is a record deficit around GDP. Compared to the WTO results ($858 billion), the information is difficult to verify, as most countries make up data to appear more solvent and to avoid being penalised by the financial market.

The balance of payments as a whole reflects the economic health of a country. The data reflected serve as an analysis for both commercial and financial decision-making.

If we analyse the statistics of the balance of trade, we can find out the main importing and exporting countries of a certain product, which allows us to know the competition we are facing. We can also find out which countries export our product. This analysis at a global level and over a period of several years will help us to develop the life cycle of our product. When a company decides to invest abroad, it must evaluate the financial solvency of the importing country through the evolution of the balance of payments. A country with a persistent deficit in its current account balance is buying more goods and services abroad than it sells abroad; if these deficits are not compensated with capital goods, there will be a systematic loss of foreign exchange leading to currency devaluation and exchange control measures. In such a situation companies may find it difficult to set prices in the currency of that country and will prefer to set prices in their own currency or in a foreign currency (sterling).

We may also have difficulties with the repatriation of profits when we establish ourselves in such countries. All this information can be analysed by looking closely at the balance of payments. The Balance of Payments (Current Account and Capital Account) of Spain for March 2011 presented the following situation:

➢ Current account deficit of 5,739.3 million euros. It is explained by the increase in the trade and income deficit and by the widening of the negative balance of current transfers and by the reduction of the surplus in services (it has fallen to 1730.4 million euros).
➢ The trade deficit amounted to 4503.4 million euros, mainly due to the deterioration of the energy balance, which increased by 20%.
➢ The income balance was negative at 2242.4 million euro and the current transfers balance recorded a deficit of 723.9 million euro.

3.5. EXTERNAL TRADE INDICATORS

The economic indicator is a measurement magnitude that allows the analysis of a country's economic development. We can say that the indicator is a mathematical operator that generates a macroeconomic index.

Trade balance. It is defined as the difference between a country's declared exports and imports during a period. This covers all particular goods, sectors or products. When exports exceed imports it is called trade surplus. If imports exceed exports, it is called a trade deficit.

External coverage ratio. It is usually valued in value or in volume, although value is usually preferred. It can be compiled for all goods, industries or individual products. Equilibrium is reached at the level 100 which indicates the equivalent amount of exports and imports. Therefore, the coverage ratio could be defined as the ratio of exports to imports of goods in a period.

$$Tc = \text{Coverage rate}$$

$$\Sigma X = \text{Sum of exports}$$

$$\Sigma M = \text{Sum of imports}$$

$$Tc = (\Sigma X / \Sigma M) * 100$$

Market shares. They are applied to measure the export share of a country in the total imported by another country. They are calculated by dividing the value of exports to a market by the total imports of that market in a given period of time. Depending on the case, quotas are calculated for goods only or for goods and commercial services.

$$Cm = (\text{Value of exports} / \text{Value of imports}) * 100$$

The rate of openness of an economy. This is an indicator that makes it possible to evaluate a country's openness to the outside world. It is the ratio between the arithmetic mean of exports and imports of goods and GDP. This index provides data on a country's dependence on the rest of the world. The openness rate reveals how open a country is in its trade exchanges. Today, China is developing a high rate of openness.

$$Ta = \text{Opening rate}$$

$$\Sigma X = \text{Sum of exports}$$

$$\Sigma M = \text{Sum of imports}$$

$$GDP = \text{Gross Domestic Product}$$

$$Ta = \{[(\Sigma X + \Sigma M) / 2] / GDP\} * 100$$

Import penetration rate. This index measures the competitiveness in a domestic market of any country. It assesses the proportion in which a country's domestic demand for imported or domestic goods flows. We can know the purchases made abroad relative to the consumption of the domestic market by defining domestic production (P.I.B.) plus imports minus exports. The denominator will be the domestic demand.

$$Tp = \text{Penetration rate}$$

$$\Sigma X = \text{Sum of exports}$$

$$\Sigma M = \text{Sum of imports}$$

$$GDP = \text{Gross Domestic Product}$$

$$Tp = (\Sigma X\ /\ GDP + \Sigma M - \Sigma X\ ) * 100$$

Export effort. Defined as the share of total exports of goods and commercial services in GDP.

$$Ee = \text{Export Effort}$$

$$\Sigma Xbs = \text{Sum of exports of goods and services}$$

$$GDP = \text{Gross Domestic Product}$$

$$Ee = (\Sigma Xbs\ /\ GDP) * 100$$

Foreign Trade Ratio. The Foreign Trade Ratio can be defined as the ratio of the sum of imports and exports relative to a country's GDP during a given period. As a consequence of the relative growth of extra-territorial trade in relation to world commodity production, trade for individual economies is becoming increasingly important. This is manifested in the increase of foreign trade quotas. This quota refers to the opening of markets, but has little reference to the competitiveness of an economy.

$$Cc = \text{Foreign Trade Quota}$$

$$\Sigma X = \text{Sum of exports}$$

$$\Sigma M = \text{Sum of imports}$$

$$GDP = \text{Gross Domestic Product} \quad Cc =$$

$$[(\Sigma X + \Sigma M\ )\ /\ GDP] * 100$$

Terms of Trade (TOT). It is also called terms of trade in which we can analyse the terms of trade with the outside world. It is equivalent to the international equilibrium relative price, which is determined by the variations in the price structure of imports and exports.

RtI = Time-Based Terms of Trade X = Exports

M = Imports

PoX = Realised price in the period 0 (base year) for the export

PfX = Realised price in period f (reference year/year) for the export

PoM = Price achieved in period 0 (base year) for the import

PfM = Price achieved in period f (reference year/fiscal year) for the import

$\Sigma PfX / \Sigma PoX$ = Exports (X) $\Sigma PfM / \Sigma PoM$ = Imports (M)

$RIt = [(\Sigma PfX / \Sigma PoX) / (\Sigma PfM / \Sigma PoM)] * 100$

If the TOTs are higher than 100, it means that the average relative evolution of export prices is favourable with import prices. If the result is below 100, the opposite is the case, but it should be noted that the representative value of TOTs depends on the price indices applied and on the influence of structural changes of the goods as well as territorial changes.

CONCLUSIONS

The development of the more industrialised countries has led to an increase in the consumption of raw materials and semi-finished products. The growth of commodities has outpaced the growth of production. In a global market, the interaction between countries is becoming closer and closer. We can speak of the "butterfly effect".

Adam Smith presented the advantages of free trade in The Wealth of Nations (1776), but limited himself to saying that goods would be produced wherever costs were lowest. David Ricardo's Principles of Political Economy and Taxation (1817) laid the theoretical foundation for explaining the advantages that countries can achieve through international trade. It was Mill who explained how advantages are distributed between countries. In the Hecksher-Ohlin Model, countries tend to import goods that are intensive in the factors in which they have a scarce supply and to export those intensive in the factors in which they have an abundant supply. In Brander and Spencer's theory, they developed a model that attempted to explain how the governments of nations where firms operating in oligopolistic markets are located may have incentives to pursue an active and aggressive trade policy in order for the domestic firm to capture the largest possible market share (bordering on monopoly), thereby increasing national welfare by increasing the profits of domestic firms. Product life cycle theory is a dynamic model that shows how a country's competitive advantages change as the product progresses in foreign markets. The life cycle model of a manufactured product goes through four main stages: introduction, growth, maturity and decline. With regard to the indicators that we must consider in order to analyse international trade and which countries are most receptive to our products, i.e. a macro and microeconomic analysis, the most important ones are a country's balance of payments, which reflects the most exhaustive analysis of a country's international trade activity and flows with the rest of the world, and some other indicators such as trade balance, coverage rate, openness rate, TOT, etc.

International trade today is increasing year by year in volume due to globalisation. In the last decade there has been a very significant growth in world trade, except for the years 2007 and 2008 when it declined drastically. The volume of international trade is around 5 to 6 trillion dollars annually. Globalisation is a theory whose aims include the interpretation of the ratios and events that are currently taking place in the fields of development, the world economy, social scenarios and cultural and political influences. Some of the reasons for the growth of international trade are political and economic stability. We are immersed in the era of communication and technology, so advances in logistics and technology bring speed and security to commercial and financial exchanges. We can also highlight the homogenisation of consumer tastes, since the tendency of companies is towards the standardisation of products for a world market with similar tastes.

ABOUT THE AUTHOR

José-Nicanor Pinilla Barcelona comes from a village in Zaragoza, Spain, Brea de Aragón, where shoes have been manufactured for generations. This has influenced his business outlook and entrepreneurial spirit. He has a business career of more than 30 years, and as a teacher and consultant in international trade, since learning by teaching is his main vocation. For more information visit his LinkedIN profile: https://www.linkedin.com/in/escueladelemprendedor/